M000311658

Praise for *Lifting Stones*

"*Lifting Stones* is a tender artistry.

This poetry is an unfurling of wings, and a fanning out in every heartfelt direction, reaching all of life's heights and depths. There is humility and there is enormous bravery. Within the pages of *Lifting Stones* there is no finite limit to Stanfield's poetic skill, nor to his quality.

He owns the journey that is *Lifting Stones*. He owns it with 'bare courage and risk' — his words — and to read this book is to step from one stone to the next in the sometimes calm, oftentimes tumultuous river that he has forged between its covers...

It's difficult to do justice to the raw tenderness of *Lifting Stones* without falling into cliché. Suffice to say it is a singular collection of clarity, warmth, grief, humour, agony, mortality, recollection, despair, and rebirth. It is an expedition, not a journey's end. It is a unique work of life via poetry, a kaleidoscopic gallery of this poet's genuine experience laid bare. Stanfield writes with a dignity. He writes with a frank self-respect that is, to borrow his exquisite words, 'eternally becoming.'"

—Mandi Greenwood, author of
Six Steps Down, Caught Inside, and *The Silver Renoir*

"Doug Stanfield writes of love and grief and of a kaleidoscope of emotions in between.

He is a deft and sensitive chronicler of the human condition and of the world we live in, crafting poetical images with great sensitivity and skill. He writes of the journey we all take and the memories of those journeys and the lessons learnt. There is a saying: 'what is man but a repository of memories?' Stanfield documents the journey in words to remember."

—Iffat Shah, physician and writer

"The first time I read *Lifting Stones*, I did so like a fresh pancake of Silly Putty just out of its egg; guileless-ready for whatever impression these pages left as I pressed into it. The second time, I was a returning tourist, dying to revisit all the amazing feelings from my unforgettable first trip to a lucky-find destination. Time three, I'm an excited child; tucked in, and barely able to contain my answer to the inevitable question, 'What story do you want tonight?' And there will be more. Stanfield's poetry is consummate storytelling: heartbreaking, funny, authentic, and masterfully crafted. And this beautiful collection of memories, musings, and hopes, has brought me back to a too-often neglected art form, possibly more necessary now than ever."

— Kat Mullaly, Toronto actor, producer, director and creative-for-hire

"I love that amid the clear-eyed Mary Oliver-ish lyricism of Doug Stanfield's poems, there are lines like: '...older men and women bring experienced stupidity to the bed.' This is the work of a man who has lived, and learned—and continues to do so with both strength and vulnerability. 'I'm not brave,' he writes. But he is. 'I'm tired of being a grown-up,' he writes. There is no weariness to these poems. They sing. They shine."

— Lauren Kessler, author of ten works of literary nonfiction

LIFTING
STONES

LIFTING STONES

POEMS BY

DOUG STANFIELD

Rootstock Publishing
Montpelier, VT

First Printing: 2021

LIFTING STONES Copyright © 2021 Doug Stanfield

All Rights Reserved.

Release Date: June 8, 2021
Softcover ISBN: 978-1-57869-058-9
eBook ISBN: 978-1-57869-059-6

LCCN: 2021902970

Published by Rootstock Publishing Poetry Series
Editor: Samantha Kolber
an imprint of Multicultural Media, Inc.
27 Main Street, Suite 6
Montpelier, VT 05602 USA

www.rootstockpublishing.com

info@rootstockpublishing.com

No part of this book may be reproduced, stored in a retrieval system, or transmitted in any form or by any means, electronic, mechanical, photocopying, recording, or otherwise, without the prior written permission of the author, except as provided by USA copyright law.

Interior and cover design by Eddie Vincent ENC Graphic Services
(ed.vincent@encirclepub.com)

Cover art courtesy of Shutterstock

Author photograph by Journey Melson, Tacoma.

For excerpt permissions or to schedule a poetry reading, contact the author at dougstan@gmail.com

Printed in the USA

ACKNOWLEDGMENTS

I remain grateful that a few poems in this volume have appeared in:

Austin Poetry Festival
Central Coast Poetry Shows
Spillwords Press
When Time and Space Conspire (LTA Written Word Series, volume 7)

And a small number, extensively rewritten and, in some cases, reimagined, come from earlier work published on my blog Hemmingplay.com and under my name in these two previously published works:

I Came From A Place of Fireflies (Hemmingplay, 2017)
Snowflakes and Ashes (Gatekeeper Press, 2018)

These writers inspired me, encouraged, taught and, sometimes, shamed me into doing as much work as necessary to continually strive to be as good as I can be:

Carl Sandburg
ee cummings
Robert Frost
Louise Erdrich
Mary Oliver
Hermann Hesse
Louise Glück
Jim Harrison
Shakespeare
Walt Whitman

Peter Matthiessen
Czeslaw Milosz
William Wordsworth
John Keats
Robinson Jeffers
Frank Bidart
Alfred, Lord Tennyson
Emily Dickenson
W.B. Yeats

To my sons, Ben and John.

CONTENTS

MEMORIES

Memory	1
Silences	2
Love in the Time of Corona	3
A Modern Man	4
Blue Gravity	5
Roses and Thistles	6
Island Nights	7
Cowgirl	8
Too Anything	9
The School of the Electric Fence	10
A Slender Thread	11
Home	12
Vanities	13
Memories over a Glass of Wine	14
Too Much	15
Waiting for Heaven	16
Blood	18
Want	19
A Fantasy of Permanent Youth	20
Why Won't They?	21
Lenny	22
Racing the Sun to Kankakee	25
Savor the Sweetness	28
Broken	29
Borrowed Dust	30
Singing Sands	31

GRIEFS AND LOSSES

Lifting Stones	35
Packing for the Trip	36
Upstream Is a Dream	37
As It Was	38
Lazarus	39
An Instant	40
Dig Me a Grave in the Air	41
A Mortal Wound	42
Epitaph	43

Ordinary Days   44
And So It Begins   45
Whatever Happens   47
Umwelt   49
Spring Was Late That Year   51
Everyone Has a Story   52
Reluctant Spirit   54
It Was the Sound   55
Standing   56
The World's Longest Epitaph   57
That Morning   58
Secrets   60
Free, at Last   61

TURNING POINTS

A Message in the Stars   64
Morning   65
Cold Silence   66
Deep Time at Mohenjo Daro   67
Summer Sounds   68
Touching Glass in the Crowd   69
A Toast   71
Epiphany   72
Close Calls   73
A Fierce String   74
At the Boundary   75
Notes from the Apocalypse   77
A Few Lines   78
Forgive the World   79
Long Walk   80
Servant to the Muse   81
Still Able to Get Lost In a High Blue Sky   82
11th Spring and Summer of the War   84
The River Is   85
Boomer's Elegy   86
Wayfarers   88

Notes   89

Memories

MEMORY

Memory is the dusty, not-quite-living museum of our lives.
You're not condemned to remain what you already are.
You may change, grow, and split the hardened
carapace of a self that no longer fits,
and like the seven-year locust,
climb high into a tree and
claim your rebirth.
But first comes
bare courage
and risk.

SILENCES

What an odd boy, they used to call me.
But what am I to do? I'm a writer, my dear,
and not right in the head.

But I do know how
to take my time and listen,
sitting under the willow tree in the spring as the birds
bring me happy messages.

I take my time with other important things, too,
so lay your warm
curves of water beside me.
If I please you,
you may pay me back with your
second sight,
and tell me where my
true nature hides,
where my pain
scuttles unhealed,
my illusions fester.
I will love you all the more for it.

For the moment, we watch the
jet stream shove the clouds
across a sky temporarily empty of jets,
the frenzy and acquisitiveness paused.
We see again the color of the sky,
realize the stars are still there
even at noon.

LOVE IN THE TIME OF CORONA

I've grown tired of disappointing women.
And of being disappointed in them.
I need a break.
I'm hiding out from a virus,
sheltering in place and
eating frozen vegetables.
Afraid this might become permanent.

I had a long life with a woman
who died several years ago,
a life better than some, I think.
Younger people have their difficulties,
stemming mostly from being naively stupid,
but older men and women bring
a lot of experienced stupidity to the bed, too.

She may be nursing grievances,
tries hard to see me as a perfect version
of what she'd missed with the
hated ex, or her dream child.
It's an old habit, born of fear.
None of this "live in the moment" bullshit for her!
I cannot win this game.

And I'll try to believe she's
a sweet, innocent maiden, surrounding me like
a spring breeze, undemanding, kind,
there to guide me to new certainties.

She looks in the mirror, however, and knows
she cannot win this game, either.
So, a pause. Which is wrong:
The reality or the expectations?
Who said age brings wisdom?

A MODERN MAN

I walk in the mists of a cold canyon,
sometimes accompanied by my late wife.
She's silent, amused, soon to go again,
impatient with me for
hanging onto melancholic vapors
when it's obvious—to her, anyway—that
I haven't wised up yet.

She knew. We talked about it at the last.
She told me to find someone.
Knew I would only trust kindness,
the warmth and secret wetness,
the round softnesses I could hold,
the friendly curves, the mysterious eyes;
she knew that all man's scripture
could be held on a 3-by-5 card,
if he weren't so stubbornly drunk on himself.

BLUE GRAVITY

In the kingdom of clouds,
vast continents of mist
dwarf the mountains,
lumber lightly
in from the ocean,
float improbably, silently.
Sometimes, when the air is cold,
they spill acres of crystal
in the high fir,
burying trees and crags in glamor.

They sweep and swell on,
break apart and spill
mighty rivers and silver lakes,
wash the air clean and
sift down through the willow tree,
bit by drop, sink from sight and
hurry to refill the ocean.

ROSES AND THISTLES

I've disappointed a few.
A few have returned the favor;
I'm angry for a while at both of us, but
also wonder if I'm usually wrong
to expect more.
My beard is grey, but inside
is the restless spirit of Ulysses,
yearning to go down
again to the sea in ships.
But from somewhere—
is that a bird? Or merely
the cry of a frightened child,
longing to be gentled
with the soft comforts of
undemanding love?

ISLAND NIGHTS

Full moon sliding fast,
light enough to read by,
be burned by,
slipping bright and cool
to the west, painting
a wrinkled, twinkled streak
on darkened waves.

As the moon waned
a little more each night,
so did the magic.
They couldn't hang on.
Little gaps grew, doubts fed
beneath the swish and boom of surf.

Too hot for clothes in the moonlight,
too hungry for each other to need them at first—
sweet & natural, a beautiful coupling.
But the price was a loss of control.

No vulnerability without trust,
no trust without truth
no truth in a tight grip.

COWGIRL

I encountered the electronic ghost
of a Colorado woman, once.
Her marriage was coming apart:
her husband had lost interest and sunk
into cruelty and betrayals.

She writhed and wrote the truth of her pain,
touched me with her anger and anguish.
She painted lurid images
of what she wanted from me,
full of anger, fury, revenge.
It drove her insane, for a time,
and she almost thought that was her truth.
Then I found an email address a year ago and asked:
"How are you doing?"

She's working in a small church in Nebraska,
making a difference, touching lives.
Her children are almost flown.
I still sense a whisper of sadness
around the edges, but who among us
doesn't know that feeling?
Life takes more than our youth,
and we live with the aftermath,
making sense of it as we can,
hoping to make a difference,
grateful when the nightmares fade.

TOO ANYTHING

She said something was too hot,
too slow,
too fat,
too skinny,
too long,
too short,
too near,
too far,
too messy,
too loose,
too tight,
too much,
too little,
too soon,
too late.
We were too drunk. Too stoned.
Then, in the afternoon, too sober.

But it was not, and never would be, too anything.
Except, maybe, too unkind.

THE SCHOOL OF THE ELECTRIC FENCE

Navigating love is a little like
the electric fence I used to
crawl through as a kid to get to the woods.
You have to be cautious, not timid.
You learn how far your bits stick out.

With both, you learn hard lessons.
You learn the difference between
fantasy, habit, laziness and reality.
You learn good intentions may be punished
for no apparent reason.

You finally learn how it feels
to be knocked silly with almost no warning,
and find yourself lying, alone, on your back,
stupefied, staring at a cloud that resembles
Winston Churchill on a bad hair day.
And even that
seems normal.

A SLENDER THREAD

Why did we have to meet like this?

different time zones
different continents
different days
different sunrises, sunsets,
different lives
different air
different seasons.

Connected by a silver
thread across many lifetimes,
a strand so fine
it is invisible
except on clear nights
when the moon is full
at *ha'passed* nine,
when the cool starlight
strums it just so—
it hums
with a quiet, sad tune.

HOME

I can't go home, not yet.
Home is still moving.
When it stops, maybe I'll rejoin it.

But this moment is real;
I can feel your lips,
and join you with
joy and easy passion.
I know the heat, the
weight, the wetness of you
in the dark, or pressed against me
at the ferry, oblivious
to jealous eyes,
saying a goodbye,
wordlessly telling
me what feels right.
Sensing it would not last.

My separateness
melts in the natural
grace of you.
Stay with me, dancer.
Until you must go.
For these last precious moments.
Let's walk on the sand,
look in the waves for courage,
for patterns, connections,
    and partings.
We'll stroll to breakfast
sit in the temporary
coolness, watching
the unworldly turquoise
of the sea, knowing the tide
                always ebbs,
but, with luck, might come again.

VANITIES

Feel your belly button,
where you were attached to
your mother.

Try not to think about
the night you were conceived.
Maybe it was a result of
a hand up a skirt, urgent kisses
fevered promises, premature explanations
on your mother's couch.

What does it matter now? You're here.
Don't screw up.
That's what it comes down to.

Or wind your watch forward
a thousand years.
Was there ever a coffin
built to last the whole trip?
We could ask Tutankhamun, I suppose,
but he's not picking up.

What does all the flash and polish matter?
At some point, there's no Better Business Bureau,
and no one left to care
whether you got the
deluxe bronze model
with white satin interior.

MEMORIES OVER A GLASS OF WINE

You weren't my first summer girl—
But were the first to take me over
Body and soul (I admit,
It wasn't all *that* hard to do).

Here's a wistful toast
To our being so young and eager, so serious, so clumsy,
So lost in hormones and music on the radio.
Sitting on the lawn under a black sky sprinkled with stars,
Fumbling, clutching, giddy with freedom, while
Bullfrogs' song charged the humid darkness with need.

I could always find your lips in the dark, ready,
Curious, eager, as glad as mine,
And we both bubbled at this secret joy we'd found.
The years have not all been easy, for either of us,
And our paths never crossed again.
I wonder about you sometimes,
Hope you remember, a little,
The innocence and joy.
And, if you do, I hope you raise a glass
With a smile, and think kindly of me, as I do you,
My summer girl, in the last days of our childhood.

TOO MUCH

Don't ask too much of me.
I'm not sure I have what you need.
I must change,
I might come up short,
Might not have the strength it takes.
What if I'm not who you think I am?
What if fear takes me?
What if I can't find courage?

I make excuses,
I'm haunted by night worries,
Imagined illnesses.
I'm not brave.
I'm tired of being a grownup.
I'm tired of figuring stuff out.
You figure it out.
I'll be down here on the floor,
Holding my breath and pouting.

WAITING FOR HEAVEN

Lonely souls,
hopeful of attention, float into
Jackson Square, New Orleans,
on a random Saturday morning.
Jock and Michelle
play a mix of the classics
in the next patch of shade.

Lovely Michelle on the violin, and
Jock, recently of Columbus, Georgia,
massages the keyboard.
Buffalo, the veteran and third member, hair strapped
by a black cloth band, plucks
a strain from Mozart
on a battered guitar.

His case sits open on the dirty concrete,
a few coins and bills
from a family from Iowa,
will buy one or two meals,
a share of a dump on
Decatur Street, when he's
not enjoying the wonders
between a girlfriend's thighs in
a ratty old apartment in the Tremé.

This trio, assembled for the day,
seem barely out of high school.
Each wandered to NOLA
to live the mythical life of music.
The joy of it: happy
with friends, content to live
rough, running from gig to gig,
earning a street corner on Thursdays
to seduce tips from tourists,

getting thinner, gradually
realizing that love alone
does not feed the bulldog.

But oh, there are times,
as tourists walk by, thick air moving
into the square from the river,
the magnolias in bloom,
the smell of overflowing
dumpsters, sights of junkies sliding
along the alleys, looking to score.

And then almond-eyed Michelle,
long black hair gathered in a bun,
bare arms in a small black dress,
raises the violin her father bought
in some far-away suburb.

She closes her eyes and begins:
the voice of angels fills the square,
moves among we the lost.
The ache and purity of the sound freezes
everyone, even the junkies, souls seized
by something holy,
just for a minute.

Blood

The needle slips in,
my body's alarmed.
Vital fluid
fills vials.
I am lighter
by a few molecules.
A bit of my spirit has left.
The vials move
down a hall on a cart,
glad of the adventure.
They spread their knees,
wantonly surrender
all the secrets
of a life plagued
by carbohydrates.
Betrayed, I say nothing.
My doctor cares nothing about
how my nose probably comes from
a man whose 35th great grandfather
was a Viking. How
he wrote poetry after every battle,
his blood, and others',
drying on the grass
in the shade
by a foreign river.

WANT

I wanted to be Steve Jobs.
I wanted to sleep with Joni Mitchell
    and have her write about losing me.
I wanted to be Leonard Cohen.
I wanted to be Carl Sagan,
Bobby Kennedy.
I wanted to be that person they'd say,
"Whatever happened to that guy?"

But that's not happening.
I'm too late.
I missed the turn,
the note slipped under my door—
or didn't have the guts—so, now,
I'm sitting in traffic on a Friday afternoon,
listening to early Joni,
bleeding on the knife edge of her words,
knowing what she had,
what Leonard had,
knowing that sort of gift
did not drop down my chimney,
or plop into my oatmeal.
The light turns green and I
turn right, with the others,
for home.
I have to mow the lawn tonight.

A FANTASY OF PERMANENT YOUTH

I'm racing the inevitable,
my only weapon
an optimistic fantasy
of permanent youthfulness.
The 1970s are to blame.
My generation is to blame.
We started this crap,
pretending we could stay as children.
In my head, I'm still about 32.

In reality, I get winded
climbing a flight of stairs.
My curmudgeonly GP—
he's been staring at my charts for 30 years—
doesn't bother with happy talk.
He grumbles and issues dark warnings
about cholesterol and sugar levels,
reminds me another stroke is lurking.
His pills make me ache and feel old.
I'm thinking of offering to sign
a release of liability for him.
He did the best he could with defective material.

WHY WON'T THEY?

"Why won't the saints look at us?"

"Even saints need a break sometimes, Honey."

"Is it that bad?"

"Yeah. It is. But try a long walk. They're saints. They'll be back."

"I hope so. I'm not sure I would."

"Me, neither. There's always a first time, I suppose. Try not to think about that.

That path through the woods to the lake is your best shot. You'd better take your time."

LENNY

Lenny was a drummer in a rock band in the late 70s. The token wild Englishman from Manchester.

The band had one monster hit and then sank without trace. The hit was played occasionally on oldies stations after a decade, then less and less. While the craziest part of fame lasted (from the spring of 1973 through the next summer) they lived the rock-star life on the road, tearing up hotels and accepting the offered bodies of groupies.

It was the 70s, when the spiritual crisis broke through into the public via the gossip columns in *Rolling Stone* and the police blotter. Lenny was known for dressing up in a giant pink cloth penis outfit and dancing around the stage, the uncircumcised head flopping back and forth, the girls screaming in the audience, tearing off their clothes. Lenny would dance for a while, then unzip the costume to reveal himself, buck naked inside. He'd throw himself, with a giant stoned smile, out into the crowd where he was pawed and treated to all manner of sexual indignity while the band played on.

Arrested numerous times for public indecency, he and the band were eventually black-balled by promoters across the Midwest and then, everywhere. The usual sequence followed: drugs, the band broke up, the lead singer had a couple of good albums, bought a mansion in Bel Air and OD'd on heroine. The lead guitarist had enough talent to play with a couple of other top bands, and then had a long career as a studio musician, had a house in Malibu, and three divorces and three children, one of whom talks to him, the other two have disappeared. The rest, like Lenny, went under and never came back. Unlike him, most went permanently. OD's. Shot and killed by drug dealers or outraged exes. Prison. Bad livers.

Lenny was an exception. About 25 years ago, after years of long decline, rehab finally worked. He got work as a roofer. He has been slapping and nailing millions of three-tab shingles on three-bedroom ranch houses in subdivisions in the Northwest in the summer and Florida in the winter ever since. Still skinny and hard as a drumstick, wearing just jeans or shorts and work boots, burned walnut brown, his long grey hair tied back with a woven string band.

He sometimes thinks about the old days, wonders how he survived, how any of them did, and tells no one who he was. Not that the young guys on the crew would care, anyway. Some burn-out musicians joined the crew from time to time, and they'd jam on the weekends before the other guys drifted away. Guys in that life aren't good at stability and normal things. Lenny was one of them. He had a truck camper and a dog, and was happy on the road.

He welcomes the sun's heat, and the precision and repetition of nailing row after row of fiberglass and asphalt shingles on, relishing the way his muscles feel tired at the end of the day, how the sweat feels rolling off his eyebrows into his eyes, and down his back, how good a cold beer tastes at the end of the day—never before work was finished, and never more than one.
He has lung cancer. Got the word last week. It's advanced and has spread to his brain, spine, stomach. He's not going to interrupt it, will let it do its thing. He can feel it in there, chewing away. Hungry. Insane. There's pain, but he has pills for that, has learned to live with pain, anyway. Just his body's way of telling him he was fucked. He always knew the day would come, just not how. It felt comforting, somehow, to finally know.

He's ready to go: Before days in a Hospice bed for those without insurance. All the tubes and the drugs, the depending on the charity of strangers. It won't be long, but even so a day in that bed would be too much. He's worked too hard to give up control now. Besides, something has changed in the world, a deeper darkening he senses but knows he can't survive. Doesn't want to. He's just tired. It's time to go.

In the time he has left, he enjoys the heat and the sweat and the labor and the beer. And the precision of the work, the rewards of being good at something physical, useful. It is April. Fort Meyers. A Friday. Finishing the roof of a new condo on the beach before the weekend. He likes getting to this job site early to enjoy the view, alone, 50 feet in the air, just him and the gulls lifting and wheeling in the onshore air from the Gulf. His buddy's fishing charter is leaving the harbor up the coast a mile or so, heading west with a gaggle of tourists going out for a few hours to try their luck with grouper and snapper, dropping lines in 100 feet of water to a sandy bottom, snagging hooks on the occasional coral rocks

He'll be on the one that goes out again early tomorrow, parked in his usual spot in the stern. With any luck, one of the pods of dolphin will escort the boat and the dads will take their sons to the bow to watch the animals dance in the bow wave, and he'll be alone. There will be a moment of solitude and that's when he'll slip over the side, the heavy sedative he's saved for years washed down with one last beer.

Dawn on the water with the soft corals and blues of the tropical sky, soft spring air tangy with salt, far from shore. He can hear the music of it in his head.

The quiet music. The closing stanza. At last.

Racing the Sun to Kankakee

The City of New Orleans pulls out of the station,
setting the ground trembling,
steel nose pointed north.
Like a thousand times before,
she finds the line away from the party,
leaving street-corner musicians,
heavenly beignets and chicory coffee.
She leaves joy behind
on parallel traces of steel.
The party goes on, the music
gets fainter, but is stuck in me
like a vaccination scar,
in my ear like an old love song, playing soft.

The train rolls on into the night, but carries the place with it.
Old Bourbon St., Canal St. with its clackety trolleys;
flood-stained Poydras, Gravier, Decatur streets.
The bars and the shops and the throngs
of sun worshipers on Jackson Square
who lounge and dance to a saxophone player
and drop coins and bills in his open case
so he can pay the rent, buy food,
play again.
They listen to the tolling of
the 300-year-old cathedral bells.
The steamboat at the dock breathes
a breathy calliope tune, luring passengers to
the Big Muddy to taste *something old, something new*
something borrowed, and some Blues.
A blond woman on her cast iron balcony above
the traffic and crowds, waters her flowers, looks
down at me and smiles. *It's OK, Honey*, she seems to say,
Life is good. Even when it's bad.
Laissez les bon temps roulez:
Let the good times roll.

The train's horn bellows long and short again,
steel wheels ticking, bumping,
roll on polished rails, gathering speed.

Number 58 follows the old line up, up,
slowing now and then but
always up, up, up, past
Metairie, Kenner, New Iberia,
hugs the shore of vast Pontchartrain,
up, up the steel magic carpet ride
in the hazy dusk, into the
purple memories of Delta country,
past fields green with winter wheat,
into the Mississippi night.
A stop at McComb, then Jackson,
then all the way up, up to Memphis at midnight.
And as we sleep, the cars rock and roll,
the engine horn blows warnings
into the darkness, the stars move slowly above.

Then morning, the conductor's voice:
"An hour and a half to Chicago.
Get your things ready. Breakfast is served."

You can see dawn a long way off in country like this.
Mist covers the fields and puts them out of focus.
At breakfast, a retired doctor traveling with his daughter
back home to Chicago join me.
Strawberries are on the menu this morning.
He remembers tending strawberries
70 years before on his father's farm
in New Orleans, in the French Quarter and how sweet
they were, how he hated
working in the beds, but loved
eating the sweetest berries in the world.
The sweetest in the world... his old man's voice trails off.

The miles glide away under the clicking wheels
as we talk, and the car rocks and rolls.
The waiter flies up and down the aisle,
used to the way the car bucks and pitches on rough spots,
never spilling the coffee.

The eastern horizon begins to glow.
We're now back to a frosty March morning.
Through fallow fields and past naked trees we fly.
And, like the Resurrection, the sun rises and claims the day,
keeping pace in the east.

Out the window, the sun's red in the mist,
running alongside us over the iced stubble of an Illinois corn-
field,
the old promise affirmed.
We race the sun to Kankakee, but in my ear
the faint music still plays far behind,
and the scent of strawberries lingers sweet.

Savor the Sweetness

We had an orchard when I was a kid:
Apple, cherry, pear, peaches.
I hated mowing under them.
The fallen fruit was full of hornets and bees;
the air all sweet rot and armed hostility.

We picked the good ones;
Dad would hand one to me from the ground
and I'd bite into a worm, spit it out. He ate another,
what the worm had missed,
showing me how sweetness and decay
live side by side.
"The good is worth it," he'd say.

Broken

In the dark the stars,
      up between distant mountains,
light a lovely path.

BORROWED DUST

This body is animated stardust.
Flitting from who knows what to who knows where.

I like how we guess about our destination, though.
It shows optimism. We're nothing if not plucky.

My own guess is that the truths
are greater than anything we've dreamt.

I could be wrong. But we're here. That's all we know.
Wait with me. Be brave.

We'll find out.

SINGING SANDS

And still the waves
    kiss the shore
        whisper secrets into sand.

The wind slides inland
    from dark seas
        from empty spaces
            haunted by silence

cold and clean,
    stroking the land
        like a wet finger
            sliding on the rim
                of fine crystal.

I might drop dead at any moment.
    But this,
        and a kiss,
            is what I'll miss.

GRIEFS AND LOSSES

LIFTING STONES

Poetry is an odd occupation: Lift
a stone to see what's beneath. Write
a few heavy, care-rounded words. Stare
at the damp past, watching secrets scuttle,
blinking in unwelcome light.
Lift the words, too, that want
to dawn with each day
and pile them in a cairn—mark
the trail and keep on, no idea if another
solitary pilgrim will chance past,
maybe years from now, pause
a moment, then reveal their own hidden things.

PACKING FOR THE TRIP

When the sun comes up tomorrow,
it won't care about our little passions,
but we'll look up, hopeful as puppies anyway.

I'm a hypocrite, knowing I'll exit as
naked as the day I arrived, but cling to
my comforts and sense of ownership anyway.
My boys will someday go through what's left,
hold up broken reading glasses
or socks with no mates, raise an eyebrow:
"Why did that crazy old man keep *this*?"
"I don't know," I'll say from the ceiling,
already starting to dissolve from the solid world,
"I thought I might need them."

Upstream Is a Dream

Time, a deep mystery with a fast current.
The past, always upstream, receding.

You can try to go back,
try to swim against the flow.

But it's no use. The current is too strong.
The present grips you, pulls you on,

and you are soon worn out, and, forced
to tend to immediate problems.

Just let the water
carry you along. It's less futile.

There are shouts and cries.
The banks are near and sharp.

The past is out of sight and mist
hides everything ahead and behind.

The water's turbulent and dark.
You can't see the rocks, the

drowned snags until you're
right on them.

Then it's up to luck and leg strength.
Sometimes you miss them, sometimes they get you.

But always the flow pushes down,
through unseen dangers, into the future.

As It Was

As it was in the beginning,
so still it is.

The hourglass turned then,
the sand measures time, again.

This is no tragedy, merely
the nature of things.

I perceive I am dying—
as does everything—but since birth.

The mayfly, the tortoise;
the orchid, mosquito. We

don't leave much behind.
Remorseless winds grind even

Pharaoh's magnificent stones to dust.
(Like Ramses, I simply can't imagine a world without me.)

It's hard to see past that.
But we ride the last grain of sand through

the passage, just wide enough, and this spirit
escapes time and space, again.

For now, I only wonder what I'm ancestral to
this time on the carousel. And: was I any good?

LAZARUS

Lazarus didn't smile
after he rose from the dead.
For 30 years, until he died again,
he was haunted
by the unredeemed souls he saw
in the afterlife.
He just couldn't smile.
His throat was always dusty
and his tongue thick.
He was notorious, though,
and played the part
with resignation.

"Come, Lazarus, tell the people
what happened to you!"
Peter would say.
John would just shake his head
and turn away in pity
as Lazarus forced words
past the ash in his throat.
He was always bone cold, though,
and sat in the sun for hours.
He bruised easily, and cuts wouldn't heal.
And there were the aches and pains
from lying on a stone slab, slowly decaying
for four days. So, it was understandable.

A miracle is a miracle, he thought.
He only wished his friend had
remembered to take him along,
away from all this.

AN INSTANT

In every life, there's a moment
when everything changes.
For me, it was the
shock of seeing your neck
as it emerged from that corduroy
man's shirt at the party.

How unaware you were at first
that our lives had just changed,
but I knew. I just knew.

"Change" is not quite accurate.
They *rearranged* themselves
like tumblers falling into place, or as
when random iron filings on paper
spring instantly into a pattern
along invisible lines of force
when a magnet is held beneath:

a new, invisible, absolute certainty.

DIG ME A GRAVE IN THE AIR

Dig me a grave in the air one day,
so I won't lie in too cramped a way.

Weep enough to let me know that you care,
but have no regrets; it's been a grand love affair.

None of us escapes life alive, after all.
There comes the time in this last port of call.

So, dig me a grave in the air one day—
or let the flames take me—as I'm already away.

A Mortal Wound

I felt for a while that grief would undo death.

      Did it?

No.
But I believed it might, if it were deep enough.

I learned something, though.
Just do this.

Go out into the desert.
Just once.
Lie down
look up at the stars,
      at a blackness so filled with gem light
      it seems alive.
Allow it to bewilder, overtake you.

You shiver, but it is not the cool air:
It is an angel who has appeared beside you.

It's then that you'll know
something
beyond your imagining
is waiting.

EPITAPH

Both doors of the world opened.
You opened them both,
passed through one as the other closed.
We heard them slam

in the storm of your going.
We bore it badly for a time

but have forgiven you
your ever after.

ORDINARY DAYS

Everything happens
on an ordinary day.
A plane full of salespeople, tourists
and families falls out
of a clear blue sky into a cornfield.
A young mother dies
on a country road after dropping
her daughter at school.

A diagnosis changes everything,
dropping without warning,
on a December day.

What will it be like
to walk these rooms
when her voice is silenced?

I wake before dawn,
listen to her breathing.
All the years
of ordinary days have come to this.

AND SO IT BEGINS

That urge to shrink
from the cool teeth of machines;
learning to endure hushed offices,
looks of concern,
competent compassion.
Maddening, imprecise precision—

> "the blood test found something, we
> need to do more tests....
> something's there...
> a blurry, thicker patch there,
> spots on bone, lung, breast, too."

Bloodless words:
> "a few places lit up"
like flying at night over Wyoming
isolated ranches below
shining with a deceptive warmth.
The needles and knives,
sensors, drips, monitors,
paper and plastic—
the whole enveloping system,

> circling, probing, injecting,
> sampling, testing, tasting

like a benevolent, curious, but
implacable, dispassionate octopus,
sorting unknowns from the known,
translating the chemistry
of death and life
into columns of numbers,
leaving it to doctors' understanding
letting them explain to us
the sudden injustice—

naked and afraid in disposable gowns—
how we   are to   live with
    this   now.

WHATEVER HAPPENS

We always knew
how it would end.
We traveled ten thousand highways—
arguing about directions—
for nearly 50 years.
And mostly finding our way.
But also getting lost.
Remember that little diner
in Wyoming where all the
locals came for breakfast,
dusty pickups nosed into
the curb outside?

Our campground
just outside of town
in a little stand of cottonwoods?
We shared 20,000 dawns and dusks,
long nights of fevers,
pain, loneliness;
passion; happiness;
the sounds of surf
and the screams of blizzard winds.
The brilliant deep snows in June
high in the Cascades,
the cobalt and green depths
of mountain lakes.

We stood on the sandy shores
of several oceans, countless lakes,
a Gulf, too many rivers and creeks to count.
We always returned to the water.
And again, now,
with salty tears reminding us
of our origins, saying goodbye.
You know the usual clichés:

"Whatever happens, happens,"
and the all-purpose:
"You never know."
There were always
the promises to keep...
For better or worse.
For richer or poorer.
In sickness...
Whatever happens, we always knew
how this story would end.

Just not when.
All is temporary.
We clutch our illusions
But it makes no difference.
I'm just not ready.

Whatever happens, my love,
there mustn't be regrets.
Such a waste of precious time.
We have walked a long path together.
We have a few more steps to go.
Hold my hand. (Give me the map).
Let's see what's around the corner,
One more time.

UMWELT

I'm a blind man inside a kaleidoscope;
A glutton with but one taste bud left;
A monk who's forgotten what he knew of God;
A tin-eared drunk waking up just as angels
burst across the heavens in song.
I'm a coma patient wrapped in wool,
strapped in a closet in a blackened room
in the back of the basement.

The blind tick only cares for butyric acid's smell—
a secretion on mammal hair—
and the exact temperature of blood—
37 degrees Celsius.
When it senses these two,
and it can do this well,
It falls into blackness, hoping
it will land on the fur
and blood of a passing deer.

The small part of the world it senses
is its *umwelt*. Nothing else is real to it.
Nothing else needs to be,
and is ignored.

For the black ghost knifefish, it's electrical fields.
For the echolocating bat, it's air-compression waves.
For us, it's a narrow band of the electromagnetic spectrum
our eyes are adapted to see, the wavelengths
that have the highest energy in sunlight.
The colors of ripening fruit and food, as it happens.
Our other senses are just good enough to get by.
We can't compete with a bloodhound's nose.
Such is our umwelt. We sense a tiny sliver of the world.
We don't know anything beyond our reality,
out of which we construct everything

like a sacred myth. What we think we know,
but do not.

SPRING WAS LATE THAT YEAR

Spring was late that year.
February and March
lingered well into April.

The daffodils,
a month late,
started to bloom
in her last days, even though she
could no longer see them.
And no longer cared.

The timing was exquisite, though,
as if they were waiting,
all rising in honor
as she slipped away.

They blazed through the week
of sadness and weeping and goodbyes,
then a few extra days for good measure.

They're fading in their time.
We move on together.
As it should be.
As she would understand.

Everyone Has a Story

A dam blocked a creek in late 1960.
The water rose, year by year,
drowned a family's rocky homestead
and for 58 years under the dark,
cool waves, bass and perch swim past
foundation stones covered in mud and algae.

A WWII bomber is hoisted from the
mud of a bay in New Guinea, and a name
thought lost to an era before
plastic was found, reclaimed.
A niece, nearly 60, gets the call,
walks into the street, cries openly.
"I don't know where that comes from,"
she tells a reporter through sobs.
"I never knew my uncle."

A neighbor in his late 80s,
feeds my dog another biscuit.
He leans on a cane, back twisted. Tells me
of a son's suicide, 15 years past.
He shakes his head. His beautiful boy,
lost over a woman, who was no good, anyway.
His broken-hearted wife died 12 years ago.
He talks about them quietly.
All alone now, he still coaches little league,
and loves dogs. "She likes her biscuits," he says
looking at a pair of bright eyes,
gives her another, and laughs.

A few doors further,
on the other side of the street,
dark-haired Michelle puts down a rake
and comes to pet my dog.
She lost her black Lab

two weeks before, and is quiet, remembering.
She glances through the dark
rectangle of their screen door,
sounds of TV filter out to the sidewalk.
Her children are still sad, too.
She just wants to touch
what she'd lost, resting her hand
in the warm fur and energy
for a moment.

All the pains and burdens people carry
with quiet dignity.
I just didn't want to see before.
They're all with me now,
and it's both comfort and rebuke.
I consider my sins anew.

Reluctant Spirit

A tear escaped your eye just now,
and you couldn't speak.
Breathing is so hard.
The words just a whisper,
as though already coming from
an enormous distance.
I don't know why dying is this hard.
The spirit in us, our connection
to the Infinite, is so reluctant
to leave this life.
But it holds hard to this body,
I watch
   you suffer
   your sisters grieve
   our friends weep
I know
   a special light is passing.
I listen
   to your breathing,

IT WAS THE SOUND

Death is not bitter;
it is a silence.

But dying *is* bitter.
With her, it was the sound.
It was drowning
in slow motion.
But at least she did not feel her body
chewing on itself, wasting away,
leaving me behind, leaving us all behind,

thousands of gasps through water, and
then more thousands.
Dying is full of the noise
of the going out, those
rising dreamy waters, rattling.

STANDING

And oh, my dear, what joy
to hear the robin's call,
the cardinal's challenge,
the excited chatter of
returning migrants, full of stories,
of tropical fruits, sunny days
and nights among the trumpet vines and
camellia on the Gulf of Mexico.
And oh, my dear, I'm changing—
a mixture of contentment,
worry, sadness, happiness and power.
With every day you're   further away
    yet nearer.

Like water, I find my level.
I've let the shovel handle fill
my hand, and bent my back
to the bloody work you left for me,
stabbing deep in pain's dark soil
'til the blisters broke, again and again.

I am here. Standing. And oh,
my dear, look: Spring has
come again after all.

THE WORLD'S LONGEST EPITAPH

This will be quick. I can't stay and can only do this once.

Do you wonder what I can see now?
I'm teasing. I can't tell you; it's the rules.

But I can tell you that all the stuff we worried
about and feared and hated is so

    utterly petty.
    It's just not important.

You'll get here soon enough.
Everyone does. You'll find out.

I did the best I could there.
I don't have anything to feel ashamed of.

I won't be back again.
(Why would anyone come back to the world after seeing what's
ahead?)

Just be kind.
Just that.

THAT MORNING

I do remember certain things,
how it was a Sunday in
April, and the daffodils were late.
How the spring sun was out and
poured through the bay windows
of our bedroom in the old house
as though nothing was wrong.
Everything was, though. You had gone.

I can't feel it now—the exhaustion
of that awful last night—
blessed by how the brain
softens things with time.
Then I remember
the hospice nurse coming at dawn,
stethoscope around her neck,
subdued blue scrubs.
She listened to the sound, looked
at my face and softened.
"Go rest a bit. She's leaving us. I'll call you when it's time."
I stumbled downstairs,
leaned against something,
glad to escape the sound of dying.
Time was short, now.
The nurse called me back.
Her heart still labored under
her poor, tortured bones,
but I knew she was already gone.

With sudden stillness it was over.
I opened the curtains to let
more sun in, confused by
a familiar scene outside that
hadn't yet noticed the Earth had moved.
I touched her cold lips,

amazed at the quiet
and stillness the soul leaves behind.

SECRETS

When the sands
shift, slide, scald at 3 a.m.,
when buried grief slithers out again,
the night holds its breath a moment, exhales.
Strange things stir, unknowns lead to
mazes, links, leaps of magic and yearning,
primitive emotions, undisguised
by convention.

There is no passion so pure
as when it springs uncensored
from the loins of an ancient earth,
in the quiet between days.
Secrets lurk entwined in the gaps of
every second on the clock,
there, then gone, then back...
neither light nor shadow, but mere potential.

Hiding in plain sight, shifting with the sand,
teasing us, daring us to pull
them into the light,
poisoning us until we do.

FREE, AT LAST

I saw my love go on alone
on a sky-blue morning.
Life in a deserted land:
A tent, fluttering in the
cooling breeze of evening.
I crawl in and fall asleep with
growing patience.

Turning Points

A MESSAGE IN THE STARS

I couldn't sleep
for the primal noise of
a trillion galaxies
blazing cold, loud,
sharp and bright.

Venus gleamed on Leo's paw.
Orion's scabbard shone; Betelgeuse burned, redly,
on his upraised arm,
Rigel arced on his sandal's buckle .

I absorbed a subtle story up there
of life, and death, and mystery,
A Mysterium Tremendum,
on a scale beyond comprehension—
in those stars, furnaces of creation, destruction,
of a power unimaginable.

I resent the need for sleep, in those last hours of darkness,
when the stars reveal such glory,
when one realizes how small we are,
yet privileged to be a part of it.
When embarrassed clouds slide toward Idaho,
before dawn touches the mountain tops.

Morning

Fog envelops morning
A misty embrace
Mysterious day

COLD SILENCE

One step into the powder,
air sparkling with crystal,
trees silent.
Two steps,
   then three,
       then more.
I stop.
Still my breath.
Ears search vainly
for sound.

Frozen trees surround me,
dusted like Yule confections,
and dark underneath, they
ignore my passing;
we walk different time lines.

Deep Time at Mohenjo Daro

Once, walking on exposed cobbles
at Mohen-jo Daro, buried for 4,000 years,
and among jumbled blocks of a ruined gate,
I stood over the revealed bones of a man.

He slept as ages passed—preserved in charcoal,
rubble and the settled debris of war,
the ruin of empire—
oblivious to all mortal things.

Is there a song the dead sing
to help pass the time?

I looked at his bones under the same sun
he walked beneath and wondered what name
his mother had picked at birth
out of the weary joy in her heart,
he who now rested anonymously in the
cool flow of Deep Time?

Summer Sounds

Cicadas, and the birds that hunt them.

A neighbor's lawnmower.

The whisper of the maple leaves in a cool morning breeze.

A dog, somewhere, barking for show.

A catch in the air, ever so faint, a momentary pause.

The whisper of the first cold front coming down out of Canada

that makes everyone feel the grief

of another year ending.

TOUCHING GLASS IN THE CROWD

The Earth burns and seas
simmer, choke, seethe,

flooding the
sticky-tacky vanities
of rich and poor alike,
from bayous to Iowa prairies;

western wilderness
incinerated by miles of
flames and smoke,
enough to change weather,
bringing true nature to
 melting, vinyl-sided pretense
 ill-suited to this new reality.

We misread the moment.

Like stubborn old Pharaoh,
one plague after another
has not broken us.
So must we lose our children
mothers and fathers,
our once-fevered fantasy futures?

The skies are not filled with clouds and rain
but signs and portents,
locusts and rising seas and heat.

We have not yet awoken; we are
confused, ignorant children.
For now, we are
condemned to wander in smoke and fog,
blindly touching our seductive
machines with the

rest of a blind world.

So pitifully, so utterly alone.

A TOAST

Raise your glass! To this brief journey of life,
to this absurd time-travel odyssey

with no fixed duration,
and no real itinerary;

to the utter recklessness of our
joyful leap into the future;

to all the surprises and pain.
To all ironies, injustice, waste;

all mysteries, all loves, all heartbreak, all joy.
Drink some wine with me, friend,

Celebrate the temporary; we have little choice.
Taste the moment and look to the next.

We plan, but God laughs.
Even a perfect snowflake melts,

and everything burns
to ash under the sun.

EPIPHANY

I knew a guy: cancer survivor
worn down by it,
to the lacy bone.
Skeletal-thin, with a dried-out look.

Still,

a light shone through
his parchment skin
like a candle through a mica shade,
a sunset of organic fire.

The brush with death had left a calling card.
"I'll be back," it said.
"You won't know when. Try not to worry."

He knew what it meant to nearly end.
But there was this glow, as though
he'd been granted dispensation to use
whatever time was left, but only
in serious ways.
As sudden as a heart attack,
he was—
    afraid of being forgotten,
    of not being *worth* remembering—
determined to try.

CLOSE CALLS

It doesn't have to be cancer
Could be a stroke, the kind of thing
you have to explain to
lucky civilians:
 "I could hear the whine of the bullet, the ugly sound
 of the predator, looking for prey."

But it misses, now and then.
You realize you've got bonus time—
you've wasted so much time.

Relief lights a new fuse ...
You mean to slap untruths.
 Make some noise.
 Burn some rubber.
 Make someone cry.
 Make someone happy.
 Be honest.
 Be true.

A Fierce String

Minute by minute
year by year
the tangled string
of seconds—
riddled with
fears of loss
uncertainties
desires
joy
jealousies
loves
hunger—
twist
eternally,
return,
drive us,
dissatisfied,
out again.

AT THE BOUNDARY

Dawn awakes later by minutes, shivering.
Does it think we don't notice?

The summer has been rainy, more than usual.
"Can't complain, wouldn't do no good," my neighbor says.

We squint up at the sky—as if a moment of somber nods would
make a difference—stroke our chins but think the same thing:

"Another year has almost gone, hasn't it?"
Regrets chitter inside, time races faster.

We don't talk about it, but it's in the backs of our minds.
We mark it most when the hours of darkness lengthen,

when the nights are cool. When the sun
rises behind stubborn clouds and fog

blooms between trees, sits in the valleys,
blankets the highways, a bit cooler.

We know what's coming, near and far. It connects us
for a moment, then it's gone, lost in thoughts

of winter's chores, and sins unconfessed
and the sweet, sweet days that slip through

our fingers like the strings of a child's balloon;
We cherish it, even as it floats away.

Everything changes. Everything must pass.
There is deep contentment in that, if we take it.

It was just after such a dawn, at the edge of the woods.
I stood in the hazy boundary light, breathing in the musk of damp leaves,

pine needles, listened to critters scurrying through
the careless litter of oak and maple and locust and walnut trees,

feeling the big pause.
The forest felt it too, and lay hushed in the mist.

The fog came last night on its little cat feet,
conjured up from the ground and the air.

I hesitated, taking in every detail.
This moment, this place, the path ahead, hidden, but inviting,

the textures of bark, the lichen and moss
on the trunks, spots of green and brown and grey, muted reds and yellows.

A great feeling welled up and tears
ran down my cheeks unnoticed, unchecked.

I was one with the moment, one with the world, on the edge
of the wood filled with mist and mystery,

like any path. Any of thousands I've traveled.
With something new up ahead, with luck.

What is was ending, the great Wheel turns
to the place from which we start anew.

The rough bark of the railing scrapes my palm,
grounds me in the Now,

I step onto the path, leaves crunching quietly.
"Where does the path lead this time?" I ask the trees.

They don't speak, but a thought whispers through the mist:
"Why don't you find out?"

NOTES FROM THE APOCALYPSE

Implausibly cool Sunday in early September.
Grey skies, temperatures barely above 60.
The sky full of smoke and ash
blowing a thousand miles over us and out to sea.
The sun a pale orange-yellow disk at noon.

All are in mourning, huddled inside,
unsettled by change and the dissolute
corruption on all sides.
Looking for meaning, finding none.
How many plagues did it take to
        almost
humble Pharaoh?
Where is he now?

The warblers, watching from the willow tree,
talk worriedly among themselves.

A Few Lines

"In this world,
we walk on the roof of Hell,
gazing at flowers."
                    -Isa, 1762-1826

"A good world—
dew drops fall
by ones, by twos."
                    -Isa, 1762-1826

Three lines may be the world.
Mountains, unchanged, ignore
temporary things, let

mists pass; there will be more.
One tardy fog-cloud
rushes up the valley,

chased by the sun.
An old man stalks by,
face set against the inevitable.

Alone now, looks neither left nor right.
Girls, once craved his
hardness, used to play

with his youthful body. Another lifetime.
Nearby, in that other world,
fog hugs cold waves on shore

beyond which scaled creatures
eat or are eaten, but can only wait,
wishing we were gone.

FORGIVE THE WORLD

Up before dawn
when the tender wisp
of dreams slides west,
a 5 billion-year-old metronome.
The same, yet never the same.
A bird —a finch, I think; I am still learning— goes about
at peace, hunting, exploring,
hopping from branch to branch
with an occasional single pure note
to let her mate know she still is near.

The Earth breathes in and out,
a promise, a new day.
The mountains—the same, yet not, I know—
please me each time
the sun touches them at dawn.
The world lives,
and so do I.

LONG WALK

I won't have power or fame.
I won't save the world.
When I'm gone, my voice
will be the first thing sons forget,
as I did my father's.

It's funny what you miss.
As the last child,
I was always playing catch-up,
the gap never closed, but
I forgave this great injustice.
It was foretold;
It doesn't matter.
Endurance comes only
    from enduring

Even asleep we partake in the becoming of the world.

I wave encouragingly at the ancestors,
2,000 generations back,
trudging north up the bank of the Nile.
You made it, old ones.

Servant to the Muse

We know dark places,
the things we daren't see
but can't escape.
Running away
is pointless,

My back is ribboned by scars
from invisible claws, from my
desperate, abandoned shadow selves.

Still, I look for the thing just out of reach.
I crave love, but choose to be slightly apart.
I love women, want them
to know how beautiful
they are in themselves.
But I still can't give myself,
can't give away parts of me again.
Not yet.
I love, but am not owned—
I am still not strong enough.

The Muse, a jealous mistress,
expects me to dance
on a high, crumbling ledge,
to risk falling and face fear.
She offers me her skin to write upon.
She's a curse, a seductress, a mystery,
a blessing.

STILL ABLE TO GET LOST IN A HIGH BLUE SKY

A 20-year-old can stroll through
falling maple leaves—
   awestruck at the aching violet-blue
   sky at the edge of space—
and live in the promise of life,
even in the mild days of
youth's Indian summer.

I remember the haze and careless
ecstasies and tragedies of youth,
of watching loved ones
and friends by the light of campfires in
nights in the country of tall trees,
all the long miles of highways,
and carefree days roaming the fields of home.
I have not forgotten.

And yet,
   all that I was, and have seen,
   all my hates and loves,
   all my travels,
   and the fear and the running,
   all had to unroll
   in this exact way
      to bring me to this moment.
What now seems inevitable, was not.
We must forgive our own foolishness.
The past is unchangeable.
The future—unknowable.

I seek things always just
out of reach
and embrace painful ambiguities,
as I must, if I am to be
an honest pilgrim.

DOLPHINS

Do dolphins envy our ability to simply breathe,
to take air in and out without thinking?
What if we, every few minutes, would need
to dive beneath the waves for life?

Swimming with languid power,
graceful, fluid and joyful,
do they begrudge the need
every so often, to slip upward and break through
the air/sea boundary, exhale, and take another breath?
Always of two worlds.

Do dolphins begrudge us our freedom?
Or is jealousy just one of our monkey traits?
They race giant vessels,
surf the wakes of ocean liners
and wreak havoc on silvery schools of
panicked herring.
Then, when sated, playful,
swiftly comes that pure joy
to slickly glide like arrows through a blue eternity, like gods,
thinking, always, of the air,
those brief glimpses of an alien sky and a burning ball
and stars.

11ᵀᴴ SPRING AND SUMMER OF THE WAR

The 11th spring of the war has stumbled into summer.
The rains fall. The birds seem oblivious to us.
There goes a pretty woman
with sandals and long legs and curly hair.
I want to call out,

"You have my heart! I have wine and cheese,
Let's celebrate this precious, brief life!"
But fear seizes my tongue and she moves on.

Disease and insanity stalk the streets.
I thought old age would be different.
I thought my people were better than they are.
I hear sounds of explosions in the distance.

The twins are heavily armed.
The flames of change light the night.
The weak are afraid.

The 11th summer of the war has started cool and wet,
but it will soon be hot and dry.
I hear more concussion in the distance,
there are more than last week.
Someone wants a war.
A virus laughs and kills.
It's always the same with us.

THE RIVER IS

in the secret places
of the mountains and marshes,
in the droplets of rain falling
alone and silent
from the tips of pine needles,
gathering in the rocks,
falling into one.

The river is,
at its source
and at its mouth,
all the same river.
As at the waterfalls,
the springs,
under the bridges,
the ferry boats,
in the rapids and
the quiet pools.
in the ocean
all at once,
only in the present—
without time,
without past,
without future—
eternally
becoming.

Boomer's Elegy

We might have screwed up...
We said love would save the world.
We faithfully sorted colors of glass and three kinds of plastic.
We took reusable bags to the grocery.
We turned the water off while brushing.
We thought everyone would do the right thing.
We thought our parents were wrong about everything;
We were partially right.
We thought rich people were smart and the smart would get rich.
We were almost always wrong about them, except for the evil ones.
We thought there were heroes (and some of us still do).
We thought we'd beaten the Nazis once and for all (because our dads
did it).
We thought our dads were wrong about a lot of things.
We were wrong about that, too.
We thought feelings were more important than facts.
We thought wishes would turn into dishes.
We thought wishes would let beggars ride.
We thought things would only get better.
We thought magical thinking was thinking.
We thought swords could be beaten into plowshares.
We thought FDR saved our grandparents and loved him for that.
We thought Ike was great, but too old for our future.
We thought JFK was cool, and that the other stuff about him wasn't
important.
We thought Johnson did some good things, but was a hick.
We thought tricky Dick was bad, then found out he was worse.
We thought then that he was *the worst* we'd see; we were wrong.
We are nearing the end and can't believe the ride is almost over.
We can't believe David Crosby has three fatal diseases.
We can't believe Joni is old and decrepit.
We thought... oh, who cares what we thought.
We were right about some things, wrong about most.
We thought we could change things, and maybe we did.
Just not all for the better.

OPPOSITES

Life happens in the space
between
                    opposites.
No exhale without
an inhale,
no breath both in
                    and out.
Order.
    Disorder.
            Slavery.
                    Freedom.
Whiskey.
Water.
A life of the senses.
A life of the mind.
Birth.
    Death.
Always one pays for the other.

WAYFARERS

I wander toward
an unknown destination.
Pretending a purpose.
As do you.

Eager to learn your ways,
how you touch,
why you sigh, where
your shy ecstasy waits.

The sunrise, the sunset.
The passing of the seasons.
New life in the spring.
A baby's smell.

Each moment burns bright,
then is gone. Another comes.
God is there.
Listen.

Happiness?
Never permanent.
Rejoice.

NOTES

"Dig Me a Grave in the Air" p. 41: This poem was inspired by Paul Celan's "Death Fugue" in *Selected Poems and Prose of Paul Celan* (W. W. Norton, 2001).

"A Message in the Stars" p. 64: The line "A Mysterium Tremendum" is from terminology developed by German scholar of religion Rudolph Otto (1869-1937). "...The central experience Otto refers to is the numinous (Latin numen, 'spirit') in which the Other (i.e., the transcendent) appears as a mysterium tremendum et fascinans—that is, a mystery before which humanity both trembles and is fascinated, is both repelled and attracted." Source: *Study of religion - Basic aims and methods.* (n.d.). *Encyclopedia Britannica*. Retrieved March 12, 2021, from https://www.britannica.com/topic/study-of-religion/Basic-aims-and-methods#ref420412.

"Long Walk" p. 80: "Even asleep we partake in the becoming of the world" is a line from "A Magic Mountain" in *The Collected Poems 1931-1987* by Czeslaw Milosz.

"Opposites" p. 87: This poem, including the lines "no breath in / and out," was inspired by this passage: "All being, it seemed, was built on opposites, on division. Man or woman, vagabond or citizen, lover or thinker—no breath could both be in and out, none could be man and wife, free and yet orderly, knowing the urge of life and the joy of intellect. Always the one paid for the other, though each was equally precious and essential." Source: *Narcissus and Goldmund* by Hermann Hesse (Penguin Books UK, 1959).

ABOUT THE AUTHOR

Doug Stanfield, the son of a teacher and a nurse, grew up on a family farm in western Ohio as part of the fifth generation to claim a history there. His family moved overseas for a couple of years when he was in high school; living in Pakistan for two years was a deeply formative experience.

He has had a few disreputable occupations, including as a newspaper reporter and editor, editor of publications and public relations in higher education, and as a department director. He is trying to atone for any sins with poetry that tells true stories, and true stories that read like poems. More honest occupations along the way have included building stone walls, working as a construction laborer, a teacher, waiter, and lifeguard. He is now a volunteer at his local hospice chapter working on communications.

While just consumed with making a living, his desire to write poetry never completely went away, even if sometimes he couldn't remember what that call had been. But at age 64, when his sons were off making their own mistakes, he changed careers again. One day, he turned on the computer, stared at the screen for a long, long time, and began.

Doug received his master's in journalism from the University of Oregon and he holds certificates from the University of London, Maquarie University, and University of Edinboro. He was a finalist for author of the year with the Annual Spillwords Press Awards in 2019. *Lifting Stones* is his third book of poetry.

Also Available from Rootstock Publishing:

The Atomic Bomb on My Back
Taniguchi Sumiteru

Blue Desert
Celia Jeffries

*China in Another
Time: A Personal Story*
Claire Malcolm Lintilhac

An Everyday Cult
Gerette Buglion

*Fly with A Murder of Crows:
A Memoir*
Tuvia Feldman

The Inland Sea: A Mystery
Sam Clark

Junkyard at No Town
J.C. Myers

*The Language of Liberty:
A Citizen's Vocabulary*
Edwin C. Hagenstein

A Lawyer's Life to Live
Kimberly B. Cheney

The Lost Grip: Poems
Eva Zimet

Lucy Dancer
Story and Illustrations by Eva Zimet

Nobody Hitchhikes Anymore
Ed Griffin-Nolan

*Preaching Happiness:
Creating a Just and Joyful World*
Ginny Sassaman

*Red Scare in the Green Mountains:
Vermont in the McCarthy Era
1946–1960*
Rick Winston

Safe as Lightning: Poems
Scudder H. Parker

Street of Storytellers
Doug Wilhelm

*Tales of Bialystok:
A Jewish Journey from
Czarist Russia to America*
Charles Zachariah Goldberg

*To the Man in the Red Suit:
Poems*
Christina Fulton

*Uncivil Liberties:
A Novel*
Bernie Lambek

The Violin Family
Melissa Perley;
Illustrated by Fiona Lee Maclean

Walking Home
Celia Ryker

Wave of the Day: Collected Poems
Mary Elizabeth Winn

*Whole Worlds Could Pass Away:
Collected Stories*
Rickey Gard Diamond

*You Have a Hammer:
Building Grant Proposals for
Social Justice*
Barbara Floersch

CPSIA information can be obtained
at www.ICGtesting.com
Printed in the USA
BVHW041427160621
609642BV00005B/1140